About the author:

Kathryn Rose Kathryn is an author, speaker and social media strategist and trainer with clients ranging from multi-million dollar corporations, to small business owners and entrepreneurs. Kathryn has a 20+ year career in sales and marketing that includes successful track record of using a collaborative mindset to increase sales. She created the first cable television cooperative marketing alliance in CT and later the Arts Marketing cooperative helping clients achieve economies of scale with limited marketing budgets.

Prior to her career in social media marketing, Kathryn was a top Wall Street sales executive, responsible for over $100m in sales per year. She used her collaboration skills to partner with salespeople from other companies to form a lucrative referral network.

Kathryn is the author of 6 books on social media marketing The Step by Step Guides to: Twitter, Facebook, SEO/Video Marketing and Linkedin for Business and The Parent's and Grandparent's Guides to Facebook. She is a sought after speaker and trainer on using social media for maximum online visibility and using online marketing and social media tools to create referral networks and to increase sales.

Her speaking events include the Massachusetts Conference for Women, Small Business Survival Summit, Ladies Who Launch Global Conference, Savor the Success Rock the World Conference. She has also spoken to school systems in Canada and the U.S. about online safety for children.

Ripped from the Headlines

Phoebe Prince, South Hadley High School's 'new girl,' driven to suicide by teenage cyber bullies

StarTribune.com | MINNEAPOLIS - ST. PAUL, MINNESOTA

Facebook photos land Eden Prairie kids in trouble

More than 100 were suspended from activities or reprimanded after being shown drinking at parties.

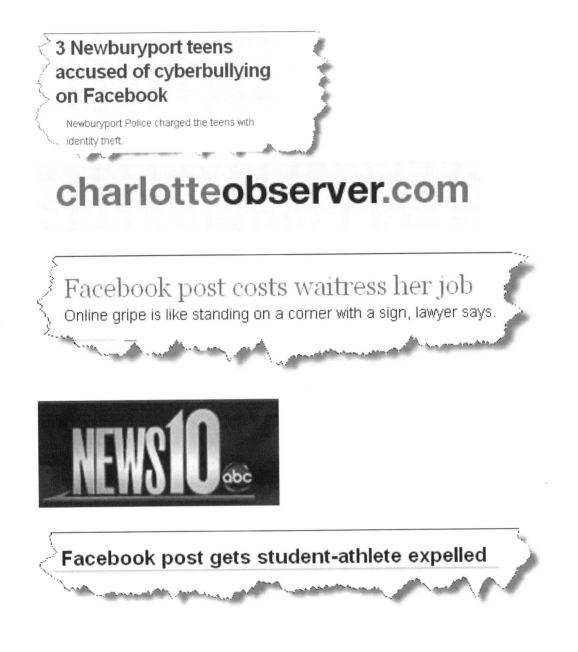

3 Newburyport teens accused of cyberbullying on Facebook

Newburyport Police charged the teens with identity theft.

charlotteobserver.com

Facebook post costs waitress her job

Online gripe is like standing on a corner with a sign, lawyer says.

NEWS10 abc

Facebook post gets student-athlete expelled

Introduction

Let's face it, if you're a teenager you probably aren't thinking about your future at this point, or if you are it's because you're about to apply for a job or college, but whatever the case, believe me, what you post online CAN affect you both now and later in life. There are also safety issues that can arise from your profile (and your life) being too open online. Many kids think "it won't happen to me" but if you just do a quick Google™ search of Facebook® and bullying, Facebook and privacy or Facebook and crime you will see the news reports that arise seemingly every day of kids harming themselves because they've been cyberbullied, kids suspended, expelled or arrested because they have bullied someone else, a kid who met someone they thought was another teenager who liked them only to find out it was an adult that wanted to harm them, or an athlete who got kicked off of a sports team because of a picture of them drinking at a party.

Teachers, coaches, college admissions counselors and future employers will be searching the internet for your interactions. Bad people will try and find information out about you. I'm not trying to scare you but if you are going to start interacting online you need to know the reality of what is going on and take steps to protect yourself.

This guide will help you to be sure you set your profile up properly so you can have fun on Facebook and not worry that the wrong people are seeing everything you post on your profile.

I originally began writing social media books for businesses and, through my research, realized that many of my friends and family's profiles were open to the public. That is when I decided to write *The Parent's Guide to Facebook*. Then as I finished it, I was approached and asked to write a teen's guide. I am not a teenager, I won't even say how long it's been since I was a teenager, but I am a mom and aunt and I have two beloved teens presently on Facebook. Even though Facebook says you must be 13 to have an account, I know that kids are joining both with and without the permission of their parents. Don't get me wrong, Facebook is a great tool that can be used to keep in touch with friends, relatives and other people around the world, but it can also have a downside, so I wrote this guide to help you understand Facebook and give you advice that might prevent you from making mistakes that could impact you now and in your future.

In December 2011, Facebook announced the roll out of a new design called 'timeline'. I have updated this book to include those features but will refer to both the old and new designs as not everyone has the new timeline yet.

Table of Contents

Chapter 1: Signing Up for Facebook

If you don't have a Facebook profile yet, make sure to read this chapter before you set one up. Even if you do have a profile already set up, don't just skip these chapters, because some of this information is really helpful.

Go to http://facebook.com,

Even though Facebook is a free service you still need to sign up. Go ahead and fill in the information requested. Many people ask, "Why do I need to put in my birthday?" Facebook has a policy that no one under 13 years of age can have an account, however, there are no birth certificate checks or parent permission slips required. Facebook works on the honor system, and believe me I know from personal experience – like the time I discovered my friend's eight-year-old's page -- that plenty of kids younger than 13 put in birthdates making themselves older in order to join Facebook. The same is true for people who are 40 and set up an account and pretend to be 14.

Once you register and you confirm your email address, you will be taken through a series of steps to set up your account.

Step 1: Find Friends

The step above requests you to allow Facebook access to your personal email account in order to invite your friends to join you on Facebook. Just skip this step. I would never recommend you give up your email list—ever. You can always go back and invite friends later.

Step 2: Profile Information

Fill out your Profile Info
This information will help you find your friends on Facebook.

High School:		Class Year: ⌄
College/University:		Class Year: ⌄
Company:		

◂ Back   Skip · **Save & Continue**

On this page, you will be asked about your school information. You are not required to complete this section or any other, this information is NOT mandatory. Facebook uses this information to suggest friends for you. I would recommend you skip this step as well, it is not necessary to provide this information and people who really know you will know where you go to school.

Step 3: Profile Picture

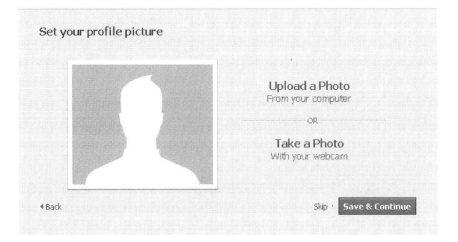

I encourage you upload a photo of yourself here. After all, it is called "face" book.

A word of caution: I've seen lots of kid's Facebook profile pictures – young girls in bikinis and boys smoking or in their boxer shorts – really? C'mon! There are over 800 million people on Facebook, do you want some freak you don't know seeing you in your bikini? That's what could happen if you upload pictures like that.

Last step: Facebook will ask you if you want to find people you know or to view and edit your profile. I will cover in detail setting up your whole profile and searching for people in the next few chapters.

Once you finish Step 3, you will come to this screen:

Welcome to Facebook, Karen.

1 Search your email for friends already on Facebook

Your Email:

Email Password:

Find Friends

🔒 Facebook won't store your password.

2 Upload a profile picture

Upload a Photo
From your computer

————— OR —————

Take a Photo
With your webcam

3 Find people you know

Search by name or look for classmates and coworkers.

Enter a name or email

5 Find people you know

Search by name or look for classmates and coworkers.

Enter a name or email

6 Control what information you share

Learn more about privacy on Facebook.

If you have already uploaded a picture, step 2 will not be visible. Before you do anything on this screen, let's move to step three and fill out your profile information.

Chapter 2: The Facebook Timeline

Before we move on, I want to touch on the Facebook upgrade to its new design called "Timeline."

In December of 2011, Facebook rolled out the new timeline profile interface and design. As of this writing, the timeline is not available for everyone. You can, however, force the conversion to the timeline once you join Facebook by going here: http://facebook.com/timeline and clicking on 'get timeline'.

If you are brand new to Facebook, you may not have the option of doing this right away.

Once you upgrade to timeline you will have 7 days to review your settings and information before it is published to the public. You can decide at any time to publish it yourself.

My interpretation of the timeline is that it is yet another attempt by Facebook to gather more personal information on all of our lives. In the old design, if you wanted to read posts I made when I first joined Facebook in 2007, you would have to go to my 'wall' and click 'see old posts' many times to scroll through the all of the information. Now, all someone has to do is click on a year and see what you posted. This can be a very big privacy issue as you may have old posts that you do not want easily accessed and displayed on the timeline.

In addition, Facebook wants you to update your profile with information such as where you were born and post things called 'life events' which is just a little creepy to me. I'm sure that is just another thing advertisers will use to target me with promotions. Nevermind the field day identity thieves can have with this information.

There are many differences to the timeline vs. the old profile. In many cases the privacy and account settings remain the same, you will just need to access them differently. I will refer to the differences as much as I can as we go through the set up.

One of the main differences is the profile design itself. The old profile just had a picture and some links, the new design asks you to create a 'cover' photo.

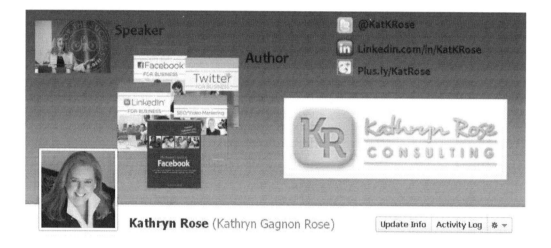

Kathryn Rose (Kathryn Gagnon Rose)

Because I use my personal profile mainly as a business tool, I have chosen to design my cover photo to reflect business accomplishments.

You can do an internet search for Facebook timeline photos and there are plenty of sites that offer free designs you can upload or you can use a photo you already have to be your 'cover design'.

How to add a cover photo:

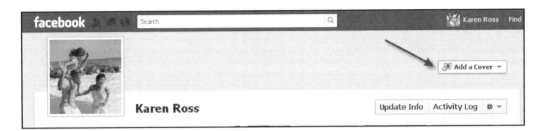

Once you have upgraded to the new design, simply click 'add a cover' and upload a picture.

Because it is not available to everyone, I will continue through the set up with the old design. I will go over the timeline setup in more detail in Chapter 15.

In the next chapter I will cover the steps to finishing up your profile using the current sign up process.

Chapter 3: Finishing Up Your Profile

I recommend that you complete your profile set up and then move on to creating your privacy settings because there you'll see the types of information Facebook can collect about you. **Entering your information in these fields is completely voluntary.** You do not need to answer *any* of the questions in this section to participate on Facebook.

If you just set up a profile or currently have the old profile set up on Facebook, click on your name in the upper right hand corner. This will bring you back to the profile page where you can edit information:

Once you click 'edit' or 'edit profile' you will be taken to this screen:

Here are the areas of information that you can fill in:

- **Basic Information**
- **Profile Picture**
- **Friends and Family**
- **Education and Work Information**
- **Philosophy**
- **Arts and Entertainment**
- **Sports**
- **Activities and Interests**
- **Contact Information**

You can access the privacy settings for your profile from here. You can also adjust the privacy levels on each piece of information you fill out by clicking the 'world' symbol or the 'shadowed image of a man and a woman' next to each category.

Facebook unfortunately, defaults to 'Public' on each piece of information. Facebook, like other social networks has what is called default settings. A default setting is one that is provided for you by Facebook in the event that you don't choose one for yourself. There are lots of "default settings' in Facebook and I will point them out as we go along. As we go through each piece of information together, I will make recommendations on privacy settings for each.

Basic Information: This section collects your basic information including a setting to control who can see your full birth date on Facebook.   Facebook's default is to show your entire birth date-- month, day and year. I recommend that you NEVER show your full birthday in your profile (see arrow on image). This is the kind of information is great for stalkers, freaks and identity thieves to have.

To change this, click on the drop down arrow and change it to "show only month and day." If you don't want your birthday to show up at all, change it to "Don't show my birthday in my profile."

You may want to just leave the day and month, because Facebook is a "social" network, many people enjoy having their birth month and date visible to friends. It's a lot of fun to receive birthday greetings and wishes on your special day. This is one of the many ways Facebook helps you make and interact with friends.

Do not fill out your current city and hometown. There is no reason you need to have this information out on the internet.

I would recommend leaving off the 'Interested in' too. Again, none of these fields are required.

If you want to, fill out the "about me" area, but remember what you say there could be viewed by those 800 million strangers I mentioned – or worse, by your grandmother! Also, you may want to leave out any identifying information like where you live or your school.

Profile picture: This is self-explanatory.

Friends and Family:

In this area you can enter information such as your relationship status, add in your partner's name and link it to your partner's profile, and link to your family member's profiles.

I recommend that you don't divulge details about your relationship, even if you are in one. If you change your relationship status a story can be posted on your wall or timeline for others to see. For example it will say Kathryn changed her relationship status to 'single'.

It used to be that once someone stopped dating you they would just stop returning your calls and ignore you in the hall, now they use Facebook to hurt each other in petty ways such as publicly changing their relationship status. It's been shown that this kind of public breaking up can cause hurt feelings, which could lead to anger, cyber bullying, and other stressful situations you don't need. So advertising your relationship status is probably not smart and is not a required piece of information.

Friends: This selection refers to whether or not your friend list is shown to other people who view your profile. If this is left 'public' anyone can see your friend list. You can restrict how others view your friend list:

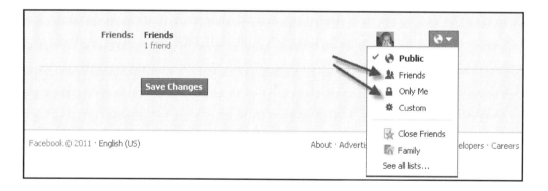

Facebook defaults to showing your friend list to 'everyone' or 'public' (See what I mean? You have to watch those default settings!) This may or may not be something you want show the world.

I want to caution you here because there was a recent news story of a case in California where a man was accused of sex crimes involving 14 girls, some of which he met on Facebook allegedly gaining their confidence by giving names of other teens he claimed he was friends with on Facebook. No doubt the man saw the friend lists of the girls.

Education and Work: The next screen to view and update is the Education & Work screen. Facebook uses this information to suggest potential connections with other students from the same schools. But let's face it, most schools don't have that many kids that you don't know or your friends don't know, so I would leave this blank as well.

Philosophy: On this screen you can choose to fill in your religious beliefs, political views, etc. Again, this is information is not required.

Arts and Entertainment, Sports and Activities and Interests: These sections allow you to fill out music, books, television shows, sports teams and topics you like, etc. This information can be used to suggest friends to you and Facebook uses it to target advertising.

Contact information: I urge you leave this blank as well. You will be tempted, and probably will, accept friend requests from people you don't know or don't know well. Letting them know where you live is not a good idea. There have been plenty of high-profile news stories about people posting their vacation plans on Facebook and then being robbed. You wouldn't post your vacation plans on your front lawn, would you? But that's what it's like when you include your full address, phone number AND tell the world through Facebook that your family is away for a month and your guard dog is in the Bow Wow Boarding House. It sounds crazy that people would be so willing to share such private details about their lives but I see it all the time and want to warn you about it. At the risk of sounding preachy, it's pretty important that some details about you and your family's life are private and not shared on Facebook or any other social networking website.

One area I want to draw your attention to is the "email" visibility area:

You may not mind if people you "friend" see your regular email address, but it might be a good idea for you to set this to 'only me' so that way, if you do friend someone you don't know, that person cannot reach out to you through your regular email address.

Viewing Your Profile

Once you are done with all of these areas, you can check how your Profile looks to other people by clicking on the 'View As' in the upper right hand corner of the screen (see below).

If you click on the 'public' link, you will be shown how *most people* (in Facebook's words) will see your profile when they visit it. You'll be able to double check how you've set your profile and correct any oversights.

As of now, all of your information should, at the very least, be set to 'friends' only so none of your personal information should be shown when you click the 'public' option.

Remember, you can always come back to this same spot, make changes and adjust.

Accessing these screens via the Timeline:

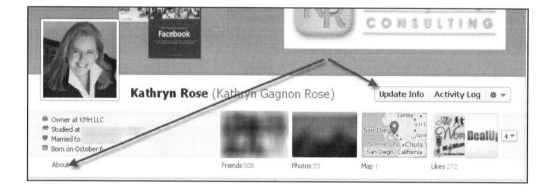

Click on either the 'About' area underneath your birthdate or the 'Update Info' link

Then click 'edit' to add or edit your work or education history:

Notice on this particular screen that the 'world' symbols have now been replaced by 'lock' icons. Click on one of these to change the visibility setting of this information.

For each piece of information collected, you can click 'edit' and go through the same process listed earlier in this chapter.

To view how your profile looks to others using the timeline design, simply click the 'gear' icon and select 'view as' from the dropdown:

Okay, now that you're done with editing your profile, let's move on to Account Settings.

Chapter 4: Account Settings

In this chapter I'll review your Account Settings, which covers the overall configuration of your account, name, user ID, etc, as well as some additional things such as notifications and language. You can access the 'Account Settings' from the drop down menu on the top blue navigation bar all the way to the right. This process is the same for both the old profile design and the timeline.

Once you click on 'Account Settings' you will land on the 'General Account Settings' page.

General Account Settings

To edit any of these settings, click the 'edit' button on the right side next to your selection.

Name: Facebook allows you to create a unique username for your profile which makes it easy to share with friends. A personal url will look like this http://facebook.com/katrose (which is my username)

If you make any changes, you will be asked to re-enter your Facebook password.

Email: you can see what your contact email looks like. This is also a way for friends to locate your profile on Facebook

Password: change or update your password here.

Networks: You can join a network of employer, school, etc. This used to be more important when Facebook first launched. Now I would recommend you just leave it blank.

Linked accounts: You can link your accounts under the Linked Accounts option, but why? It's better to keep your Facebook account separate from other networks to keep a tighter watch on your passwords. Speaking of passwords—keep it to yourself, your BFF today may not be tomorrow. **DON'T SHARE PASSWORDS**

Language: There are over 70 languages available on Facebook. You can change it to your native language on this screen.

Security Settings

The next item in the 'Account Area' menu is Security Settings. You will want to pay close attention and adjust these settings.

There have been lots of news stories about people's accounts being hacked and fake messages sent to their friends. By adjusting these settings you can greatly reduce the likelihood of your account being compromised.

Security question: if you ever have to contact Facebook, this will be the question they ask to identify you as the account owner.

Secure browsing: If you are someone who accesses Facebook from a public internet access point (i.e. libraries, coffee shops, etc.) this should most definitely be set to 'enable'.

Enabling secure browsing for an account ensures that data cannot be monitored by other users of the network or the internet service provider.

Login Notifications: This is an important area. This area was made more robust after Mark Zuckerberg's (yes, the founder of Facebook) account was hacked.

By enabling this option you will be notified if someone tries to access your account from a computer or mobile device that you have not used before. This way if someone is trying to "hijack" or "hack" your account, you will be notified immediately. In this screen shot, this person only has email set up at this time. You can set up a mobile phone with Facebook and this feature will also ask if you want to be notified via text message. If you have a text-enabled phone I recommend that you set it up so you can be instantly notified.

Login Notifications	We can notify you when your account is accessed from a computer or mobile device that you haven't used before. Choose a notification method below:
	☐ Email
	Save Changes Cancel

What if you get a notification that someone has hacked your account? Go immediately and change your password.

Login Approvals: You can set it so you will have to enter a PIN number any time you use an unrecognized device. This further strengthens your account security.

Login Approvals	☐ Require me to enter a security code each time an unrecognized computer or device tries to access my account
	Save Changes Cancel

App Passwords: If you have applications set up in Facebook, you may not be able to access them if you have login approvals enabled. This area will allow you to set up 'app specific' passwords.

Recognized devices: Once you have logged in from an outside device and approved its access (for example a spouses computer), it should not have to be approved again. Here you can see the registered devices that were approved to access your account.

Recognized Devices	You do not have any registered devices.
	Save Changes Cancel

Active Sessions: This area shows the approximate location and browser type you are currently using and some past locations you have used to access Facebook

If you see any suspicious logins, click 'end activity' and go immediately and change your password.

Deactivate account: this is self explanatory.

Notifications Settings

This is where you check off the access to your notifications of events, notices and other interactions on Facebook.

Notifications Settings

We send notifications whenever actions are taken on Facebook that involve you. You can change which applications and features can send you notifications.

Notifications are being sent to ████████ @gmail.com (email).

Recent Notifications

All Notifications

Facebook	16	Edit
Photos	8	Edit
Groups	6	Edit
Pages	3	Edit
Events	9	Edit
Questions	5	Edit
Notes	3	Edit
Links	3	Edit

Personally I like to receive immediate notifications of some things while being notified of others can be annoying. This is just a basic screen shot but when you get to the screen, you can see how detailed you can get. You can always come back to this screen and change these settings as you find out how many e-mail notifications you are receiving.

Facebook	✉
Sends you a message	☑
Adds you as a friend	☑
Confirms a friend request	☑
Posts on your Wall	☑
Pokes you	☐
Has a birthday coming up (weekly email)	☑
Asks to list you as family	☑
Suggests a friend you might know	☑
Adds a friend you suggested	☑
Joins Facebook after your invite	☑
Tags you on their profile	☑
Tags you in a post	☑
Mentions you in a comment	☑
Comments on a post you were tagged in	☑
Subscribes to your public updates	☑
Posts content (Close Friends list only)	☑
Says you are with them in a post	☑
Likes your post	☑
Likes a post you're tagged in	☑

Save Changes Cancel

Checking the box allows it, no check removes it.

I personally recommend that you always get notified when someone 'tags' you in a post (I will cover this in more detail later in the book), 'Says you are with them' in a post and anytime you could be 'mentioned'. This way you keep tabs on what is being posted about you.

You can even have notifications sent to your cell phone via text message also known as SMS. But it can get expensive if you don't have a text-message plan. Facebook messages can really build up fast, so don't check this if you want to avoid excessive text messaging charges.

Mobile: This is where you can register for mobile texts. It also verifies your information.

Payments: You can make purchases via Facebook but mostly people use this for purchasing Facebook advertising.

Facebook Ads: This is where Facebook could use your personal information for Facebook social ads. Although Facebook says here they will not use your photos in ads, I recommend that you set this to "no one".

Also, Facebook lets your friends know when you've "liked" an ad, you may not want that to be shown so scroll down to the bottom and select "no one" as well.

Chapter 5: Privacy Settings Profile Information

The question I get the most when I am out speaking to organizations, students and parents about Facebook is "what should I know about Facebook that will help me protect my privacy?"

Many privacy controls, particularly those surrounding your personal information, housed under the 'Info' or 'Profile' area of your personal profile, can now be accessed directly alongside the piece of information, as I mentioned in a previous chapter.

To access the broader 'Privacy Settings' screen go to the upper right hand corner of your Facebook profile on the blue navigation bar and click on the drop down arrow and choose 'Privacy Settings'. Again, this process is the same for both the old profile and the timeline design.

You will come to this screen:

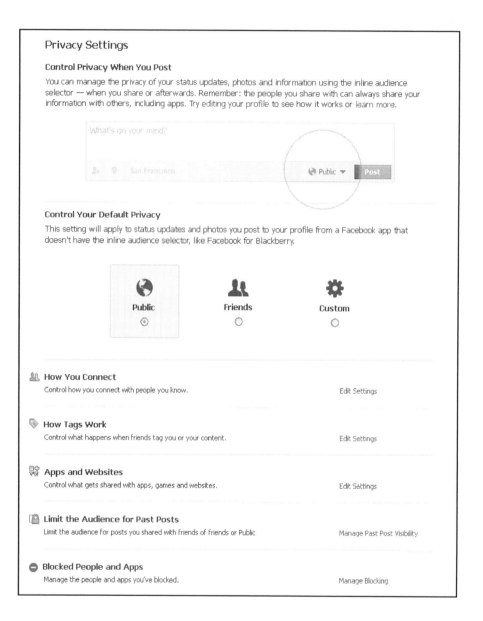

Facebook lets you know that you can control the privacy setting of each post as you make them. Users were already able to do this and be very specific about it using 'friend lists' which I will cover later in Chapter 13 but now they are making sure to point this out as you set up your privacy configurations.

Privacy Settings When Posting from Mobile Device

The next thing you will see on the screen is the 'Control your Default Privacy' option. This controls your privacy on posts made by applications outside of Facebook, i.e. Blackberries and other mobile devices. With the new privacy update you must tell Facebook how you want your status updates shared. I highly recommend you set this to 'Friends' so that your updates are not made public by accident when you post to your Facebook page from your cell phone.

Chapter 6: Privacy Settings-How You Connect

The next area on the screen deals with the privacy choices of connecting on Facebook.

Once you click on 'Edit Settings' next to the 'How You Connect' area, Facebook's has a recommended default privacy setting configuration. Unfortunately, in some cases those settings are the *least* private.

(As I said earlier, beware of default settings!) Here is a detailed explanation of the three main privacy settings:

1. **Everyone (or Public) – This is not just everyone on Facebook, this is everyone on the INTERNET.** *Facebook says, "the*

"Everyone" setting works differently for minors (under 18) than it does for adults. When minors set information like photos or status updates to be visible to "Everyone," that information is actually only visible to their friends, friends of their friends, and people in any school or work networks they have joined."

That's still a lot of people who could potentially view your personal photos and updates. So if I were you I'd check these settings and make sure they are not set to "everyone" for your profile. Most likely Facebook's own blocking system is protecting you, but why risk it?

2. **Friends of Friends** – This means all of the people you "friended" AND all of their friends. Many people don't get what this means so I want to be clear: Let's say you have not "friended" your coach but you have "friended" someone who HAS "friended" your coach. If you have your settings configured to 'friends of friends' your coach will be able to see that area of your Facebook account. So if you check "friends of friends" and you make a post about how much you hate your coach or an inappropriate picture that might get you kicked off the

team, they could quite possibly see it and you could face some serious consequences.

So now might be a good time to remind you that what you post on Facebook should always be considered public, no matter how your privacy settings are set. Use common sense and don't post things you wouldn't want others to see.

3. **Only Friends – The means that only people you "friend" can see your profile information.** Of the three, this is the most secure setting for your information. BUT you need to be careful who you "friend".

There is also the option to "Customize Settings":

How You Connect

Who can look up your profile by name or contact info?   **Everyone** ▼

Who can send you friend requests?   **Everyone** ▼

Who can send you Facebook messages?   **Everyone** ▼

Who can post on your Wall?   **Friends** ▼

Who can see Wall posts by others on your profile? (Note: Stories about likes, friendships, and some other types of wall content aren't included in these settings.)   **Friends of Friends** ▼

Learn more

> Public
> ✓ **Friends of Friends**
> Friends
> Only Me
> ✳ Custom
>
> Close Friends
> Family
> See all lists...

If you click customize, you will be taken to this screen that has these and other privacy choices:

Custom Privacy

✓ **Make this visible to**

These people or lists: Friends of Friends ▼

| Friends of Friends |
| Friends |
| Specific People or Lists... |
| Only Me |

friends can also

✖ **Hide this from**

These people or lists: [   ]

Save Changes   Cancel

If you click on 'customize' on this screen you will see that the phrase 'Hide this from' is a choice. Here, you can manually select friends that you would like to exclude.

Let's go through the privacy choices here one by one:

Who can look up your profile?

This setting refers to Facebook's internal search capabilities. It's best that you set this to 'Friends Only'. This means your profile will not show up if someone searches for you by typing your name into the Facebook search area at the top of the page. The reason for this is a simple one. It's easy for strangers to find young people on Facebook without even knowing them. For instance, if you type into the Facebook search bar a name like "Jane Smith," you will see a list of possible matches, with photos. If someone is interested in targeting young people, all they have to do is type in a name, look at the pictures and then send a friend request to you. Remember, people who join Facebook don't have to prove they are who they say they are and that 16 year old hot guy/girl you don't know who just sent you a friend request could be a 50 year old psycho.

Friend Requests and Private Messages

You may also wish to limit random people's ability to "friend" you and send you private messages.

If you decide to keep your profile available for searches within Facebook, once someone finds you they can (by default), either send you a friend request or a private message.

I get weird messages all the time from strangers telling me they saw my profile and that I'm their soul mate and asking if I want to meet. Here's an example of one I received recently:

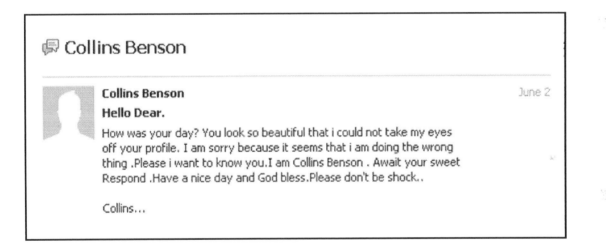

To turn off the ability for anyone who comes across your profile in a search to able to send you private messages, find the area that says, 'send me messages' and change it to 'only friends'. This way, only your Facebook friends can send you private messages.

Wall Post Privacy

In this section, you have the option to restrict who can post to your wall.

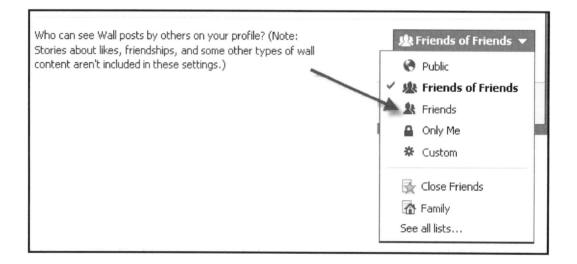

Since the whole point of Facebook is to be social and share information, I recommend you keep this set to 'Friends'.

Who Can See Wall Posts by Others

As with the 'post to your wall' settings I recommend you set this to 'Friends' this way your Facebook friends can see people who post on your wall—say for birthday wishes and the like. If you find that someone is constantly posting inappropriate things on your wall, you can simply hide them or 'unfriend' them and I will cover that in Chapter 14.

I know it's tempting to hide information from your parents but I encourage you to have an open dialog with them. Just keep in mind that's always possible to recover *whatever* you put online, regardless of your privacy settings. So while you might think you're being sneaky, I would be careful in using these settings.

Chapter 7: Privacy Settings - How Tags Work

This area refers to tags in 'posts' or 'status updates' or photos/videos on the platform. Before I cover the privacy areas surrounding post tags, I will explain how post tagging works.

Tagging People in Posts

When you are interacting on Facebook, one of the things you can do is 'tag' people you are friends with or business pages you've liked in posts. This way you can invite someone you are talking about into the conversation without actually posting on their wall. For example, you would write:

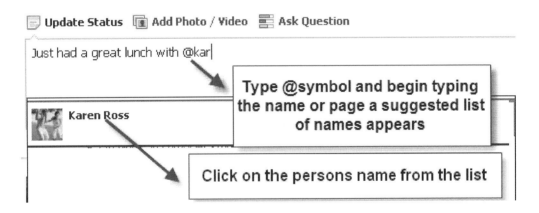

You will not be able to see it in the black and white type of this book but once the post is shared on your profile the name comes up in a light blue. This is a direct link to the person's profile or business page.

This also posts the message on the person (or business page) profile that you have tagged. See screenshot below.

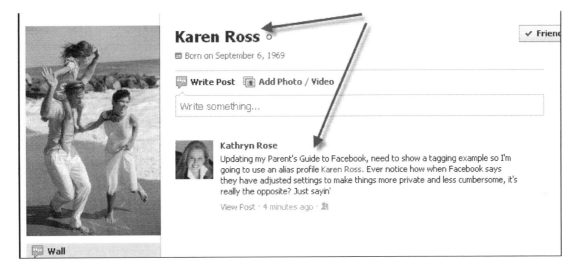

If you have the new 'timeline' enabled this post would show up on their "Timeline" instead of their "Profile".

Others Tagging You in Photos/Videos

"Tagging" is also used on Facebook for your friends to identify you in a photo or video AND to notify you that they've posted something that might be of interest to you or that includes you, such as pictures.

This makes this particular privacy setting very important. If others post photos of you and 'tag' you in the photo, the photo then appears in your news stream and profile for all of your friends to see unless you've set your privacy settings to avoid this.

I must admit that one of the things that drives me nuts is when someone 'tags' a photo of me. I am one of those people who LOVES the fact that, with the invention of digital cameras, I now have the ability to only keep the photos I think make me look good. Other people are doing the same thing, they are posting photos of themselves that they think make THEM look good, not caring at all how you look.

Now you can't stop friends and relatives from posting embarrassing photos of you if they insist on doing so despite your protests, so thankfully you can 'untag' yourself so at least the photo is not identified with your name and doesn't show up on your Facebook profile. The process of tagging and untagging photos is covered in Chapter 19.

Profile (Timeline) and Tag Review

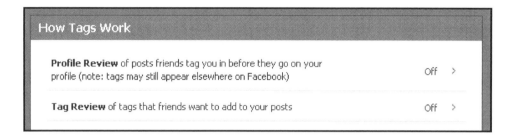

This is a great feature that allows you to review tags of posts and photos before they are posted to your wall or timeline.

With these two settings, you have only a choice whether or not to turn them 'On' or 'Off'.

In the first, you can set it so that if anyone tags you in a post, photo or video, you can review it before it goes live on your profile or timeline. You can approve or deny the request to share it with your friends.

With the second choice, if a friend wants to add a tag to YOUR post, photo or video, you can have this set to review. Again, you can either approve or deny the request.

These settings are entirely up to you. Unfortunately, you can't turn 'off' reviews for posts and 'on' photo/video tags. You may want to keep them off until you see how tags of you are being used. I recommend for kids to turn on the reviews and make sure that the pictures that are tagged of them present them in the best light. There are plenty of news stories that talk about kids being kicked off of sports teams and suspended from other programs because a picture of them drinking was posted on Facebook.

Maximum Profile Visibility of Tags

This setting refers to who can see posts that you are tagged in. I recommend setting all viewing of any types of posts on your profile or timeline to 'Friends'.

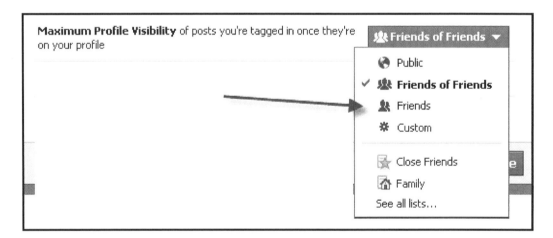

Tag Suggestions for Photos

When friends upload photos that look like you, Facebook suggests they tag you in the photo. I find this a little disturbing personally—Facebook using facial recognition?--so I keep my setting to 'Off'. But again, this is your choice.

Facebook Places Privacy

"Facebook Places" is a way to share where you are in real time by "checking in" via an application on your smart phone. You can also let people know where you are right from the platform itself by adding it to your status update:

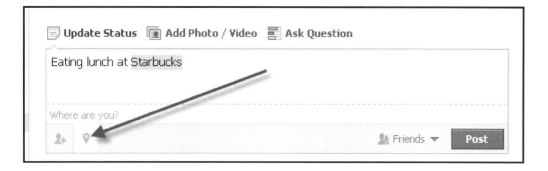

Once you click the "places" symbol Facebook asks "Where are you?" for you to enter the location yourself or Facebook uses the location of your IP address to suggest a location for you.

In the case of posting via mobile, "places" uses the GPS in your smart phone to determine your location. The idea behind the places feature, is if one of your friends sees you are at a particular place, they can come by and hang out with you.

(If you do not choose to check in, your location is not reported. In other words, Facebook won't tell people where you are, unless YOU share it.)

It is never a good idea to let people know you are away from home so I recommend you never use it. There is, however, the possibility of OTHERS sharing your location.

Two other "places" settings to be aware of:

Friends can check me into places: This setting allows friends to check you in. Imagine you called in sick to after-school job, but you're really at the ball game. Your "friend" can innocently check you in and suddenly you're busted to your boss and the co-worker who covered for you that day! Not a good thing! Disable this feature simply by turning it 'Off'.

Friends Can Check You Into Places using the mobile Places app	On >

Even though Facebook says you can remove the tag if you want to, the damage may already be done. Safest bet, disable the feature.

Chapter 8: Privacy Settings - Apps and Websites

In the Apps and Websites area under Privacy Settings, you can control what information is accessible to any applications you use, as they may publish updates in your Notifications and News Feed sections. As you make your profile settings more restrictive, less information is available to these applications.

As you will read on the screen, Facebook says:

> On Facebook, your name, profile picture, gender, networks, username and user id (account number) are always publicly available, including to apps. Also, by default, apps have access to your friends list and any information you choose to make public.

Choose Your Privacy Settings ▸ Apps, Games and Websites

◄ Back to Privacy

On Facebook, your name, profile picture, gender, networks, username and user id (account number) are always publicly available, including to apps (Learn Why). Also, by default, apps have access to your friends list and any information you choose to make public.

Edit your settings to control what's shared with apps, games, and websites by you and others you share with:

Apps you use	You're not currently using any apps, games or websites. Visit the apps dashboard or games dashboard to get started. ✎ Turn off all apps.	Edit Settings
How people bring your info to apps they use	People who can see your info can bring it with them when they use apps. Use this setting to control the categories of information people can bring with them.	Edit Settings
Instant personalization	Lets you see relevant information about your friends the moment you arrive on select partner websites.	Edit Settings
Public search	Show a preview of your Facebook profile when people look for you using a search engine.	Edit Settings

This area also houses your 'public search setting' that is how people can find your profile in a Google or other search engine search.

To begin, we'll cover the 'apps you use section'. This only applies if you have been on Facebook previously and you have a list of applications that you have used or have allowed access in the past. For example, my personal profile has 74 apps that I have added to my Facebook experience for one reason or another:

Apps you use:

To remove an app from your profile or timeline, simply click the 'Edit Settings' on the right, you will see a list of the applications you have allowed access. You can also access this privacy area via the 'Account Settings' screens from Chapter 4.

To remove them from your profile either click "Remove unwanted or spammy applications."

Or click 'Edit Settings'

Then from the list of apps, click on 'Edit' next to the apps you would like to edit or remove.

App Settings

You have authorized these apps to interact with your Facebook account:

Klout	Less than 24 hours ago	Edit	✕
Pinterest	Monday	Edit	✕
Mashable	Monday	Edit	✕
TabSite - Free Page App | Static FBML Alternative!	December 21	Edit	✕
DISQUS	December 18	Edit	✕
YouTube	December 14	Edit	✕

Once you click 'Edit' you will see the information each of the apps is gathering:

YouTube	Last logged in: December 14		Remove app
This app can:	**Access my basic information** Includes name, profile picture, gender, networks, user ID, i...See More		Required
	Post to Facebook as me YouTube may post status messages, notes, photos, and videos on my behalf		Remove
	Access posts in my News Feed		Remove
	Access my data any time YouTube may access my data when I'm not using the application		Remove
Last data access:	Basic Information See details · Learn more		2 Days Ago
App activity privacy:	Who can see posts and activity from this app on Facebook?		👥 Friends ▾

Close

From here, you can remove the app completely, or limit the functionality of the application based on the application requirements. For example, in the previous screen shot, the

YouTube application only requires me to allow access to my basic information in order to use it in Facebook. However, this application below, requires me to allow them access to my profile information and be allowed to send me email at my personal address:

If I do not want them to have access to this, I must remove the application.

In addition, you can see the privacy settings for "Who can see posts and activity from this app?" Here you can limit the viewing of each application's posts.

You can also choose to remove all apps from your profile by clicking here:

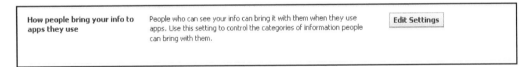

The next privacy setting you need to be aware of in the 'Apps and Websites' section is:

How people bring your info to apps they use:

This refers to how your friends can share information about YOU through applications THEY use. Click on 'Edit Settings' and you can see the types of information friends are allowed to share about you through the use of third party applications:

How people bring your info to apps they use

People on Facebook who can see your info can bring it with them when they use apps. This makes their experience better and more social. Use the settings below to control the categories of information that people can bring with them when they use apps, games and websites.

- ☑ Bio
- ☑ Birthday
- ☐ Family and relationships
- ☐ Interested in
- ☐ Religious and political views
- ☐ My website
- ☐ If I'm online
- ☐ My status updates
- ☐ My photos

- ☐ My videos
- ☐ My links
- ☐ My notes
- ☐ Hometown
- ☐ Current city
- ☐ Education and work
- ☐ Activities, interests, things I like
- ☐ My app activity

If you don't want apps and websites to access other categories of information (like your friend list, gender or info you've made public), you can turn off all Platform apps. But remember, you will not be able to use any games or apps yourself.

Save Changes | Cancel

You will want to go through this and check the information that you want to allow your friends to share through the use of various applications on Facebook (like Birthday Calendar, or Greeting Card). Unfortunately, you cannot restrict information like your friend list, gender or username unless you turn off access to all applications, including the ability to add applications yourself.

The number of applications that are available can be overwhelming to say the least. Think carefully before accepting one. These applications are free because accepting one gives third parties—outside Facebook-- permission to gather information about you and your friends that make up offline profiles that are then used to market stuff to you. Un-clicking your personal information will still give your friends access to the application, while the application will simply no longer have access to your information. In my opinion, you should not have to pay the price of your friend playing a game by turning over all your personal information.

I suggest you un-check all these items to keep your information from being accessed by these third party applications. If you have any of your information set to 'public' or 'everyone' it will automatically be checked off on this screen.

Some applications and games can be fun, and others, not so much. You'll decide through experience which ones you enjoy, and you can always delete any applications that you decide later you don't use.

The "Instant Personalization" setting

In April, 2010, Facebook introduced "Open Graph" application which they call "Instant Personalization." All it does is show you products you may be interested in based upon past purchases.

The idea is that users will want a personalized web experience so only content that matches their past likes will come up first.

What does this mean for you? Not much. The downside is that this is an application and can collect personal information about through the application, or if your friends authorize the application it may collect information that way as well.

How do you turn off the personalization? You can go to the instant personalization setting and turn it off by unchecking the 'Enable instant personalization on partner websites' box.

Choose Your Privacy Settings ▸ Instant Personalization

◂ Back to Apps

Instant Personalization

We've partnered with a few websites to provide you with great, personalized experiences the moment you arrive, such as immediately playing the music you like or displaying friends' reviews. To tailor your experience, these partners only access public information (like your name and profile picture) and other information you've made public.

When you first arrive at the following sites, you'll see a notification message and an option to turn off the personalized experience:

- Bing - Social Search
- Pandora - Personalized Music
- TripAdvisor - Social Travel
- Yelp - Friends' Local Reviews
- Rotten Tomatoes - Friends' Movie Reviews
- Clicker - Personalized TV Recommendations
- Scribd - Social Reading
- Docs - Document Collaboration

Uncheck to turn this off

To turn off instant personalization on all partner sites, uncheck the box below.

☑ Enable instant personalization on partner websites.

Public Search Listing Privacy:

The last area I will focus on here is the "Public search" area.

This setting controls whether your Facebook profile comes up in a search engine listing like Google. In order to REMOVE your Facebook profile completely from public search results, simply click on the 'edit settings' to the right of the 'Public search' area and un-check 'Enable public search'.

For children, Facebook states: "minors do not have public search listings created for them, so they do not appear in outside search engines until they have turned 18."

BUT I still recommend you check it. Facebook gets a huge amount of traffic from Google and the other search engines. Not all of your profile is displayed; only the information you allowed to be publicly shared when you set your privacy settings to 'Everyone.'

If you have misrepresented your age in order to join Facebook in the past or to access things available only to adult users, your profile could be available through a Google search. Studies show over 45% of employers and admissions counselors check Google and the social networking sites before making a decision to hire or accept your application.

As you can imagine, this is an important setting to consider so that you are not unintentionally showing all of your and your friends photos, wall posts, etc. to everyone on the internet.

You can see what your profile looks like in an internet search by clicking the "see preview" button, and again, I highly recommend checking out how your profile appears to the entire internet user base. This is how the profile of the alias page I set up looks in a Google search:

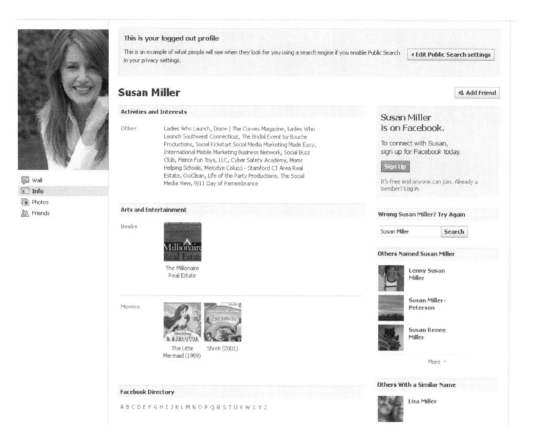

As you can see, there is plenty of information that I have allowed non Facebook users to see here.

This is an example of my actual timeline or personal profile:

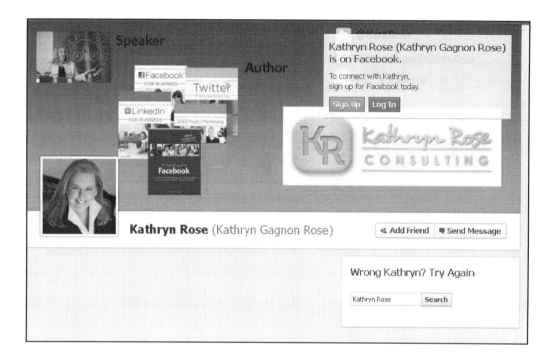

I have intentionally hidden my friend lists, my wall posts, my photos, etc. from public view so you only see my timeline "cover" image and the ability to add me as a friend or send me a message.

Chapter 9: Limit the Audience for Past Posts

When you upgrade to the new timeline, or have been on Facebook previously, your past posts may be visible to the 'public' or 'everyone' simply because the limits on privacy were not available at that time, or you forgot to set them properly.

Using the 'Limit the Audience for Past Posts' you can automatically change the audience privacy level for past posts to 'friends'. This way any posts you have left public or everyone will change to 'friends'. You will see in Chapter 15 when I cover the new timeline, that you can always go and individually change the privacy level for each post. For now, it would probably be a good idea to go ahead and limit the privacy viewing level for your old posts. Click 'Manage Past Post Visibility' then 'Limit Old Posts'.

Chapter 10: Privacy Settings – Block List and Bullying

When I was about to enter middle school a friend and I got stuck going to the one across town, not the one that the majority of our Elementary School class went to. You can imagine all of the kids in the junior high we ended up at already had cliques of friends set up. The bullying started probably a week after we were there. For two years, they said stuff about us, pushed us into lockers, "dumped" our books, harassed us on the bus and always tried to provoke us into a fight. It was a nightmare. I can't even imagine what it would have been like had we had Facebook then. Now the nasty hate messages travel at light speed for the whole world to see. At least then, we could look forward to going home and escaping their hateful words. Now, you're stuck with it 24-7 through texting and Facebook posts. It might make you think you just can't take it anymore and do something drastic like hurt yourself either by cutting or worse.

That is one of the reasons I wrote this book. When I wrote the original *Parent's Guide to Facebook* I did a great deal of research and didn't have to look far to find story after story about kids hurting themselves or taking their own lives because of the stress of being bullied online. I know from experience that this time does not last forever. But I also know if you are the victim of a bully it *seems* like a lifetime. It will pass. Please, talk to someone about it; a parent, a guidance counselor, a teacher.

The internet is the coward's stage. The fact that people can be anonymous is an attractive thing that can be used to hurt others. You can do something about it. Facebook gives you the option to actually block individual people from interacting with you.

Blocked People and Apps

Blocked People and Apps
Manage the people and apps you've blocked.   Manage Blocking

Click 'Manage Blocking' and you come to this screen:

Choose Your Privacy Settings ▸ Manage Blocking

◂ Back to Privacy

Add friends to your Restricted list

When you add friends to your Restricted list they can only see the information and posts that you make public. Facebook does not notify your friends when you add them to your Restricted list. Edit List.

Block users

Once you block someone, that person can no longer be your friend on Facebook or interact with you (except within apps and games you both use and groups you are both a member of).

Name: [   ] Block

Email: [   ] Block

You haven't added anyone to your block list.

Block app invites

Once you block app invites from someone, you'll automatically ignore future app requests from that friend. To block invites from a specific friend, click the "Ignore All Invites From This Friend" link under your latest request.

Block invites from: [Type the name of a friend...]

You haven't blocked invites from anyone.

Block event invites

Once you block event invites from someone, you'll automatically ignore future event requests from that friend.

Block invites from: [Type the name of a friend...]

You haven't blocked event invites from anyone.

You have many different "block" options but if you just want to block a particular individual, add the person's name or email and they will be blocked--which ultimately means that your profile, posts or interactions on Facebook will no longer be visible to them when searching for you. The person will NOT be notified that they were blocked.

Of course, you do have the option of 'unfriending' them as well. When you 'unfriend' someone they do NOT get a notification about it. Only you will know that you unfriended them until they try to view your page. At that point they will realize they are no longer on your friend list.

Here you can also block application invites or event invites from particular people.

In the old design, you can also report a person who is bullying or harassing you by going to their profile page, scroll down on the left side and click 'Report/Block'.

Report and/or Block This Person

☐ **Block Susan Miller**
   Blocking means you won't be able to see or contact each other on Facebook

Additionally, you may report this profile as the following:

○ This is my old account
○ This person is annoying me
○ This profile is pretending to be someone or is fake
○ Inappropriate profile photo
○ This person is bullying or harassing me

Is this your intellectual property?   **Continue**   **Cancel**

On the timeline, you will need to click on the icon that looks like a 'gear' then 'report/block' from the drop down menu:

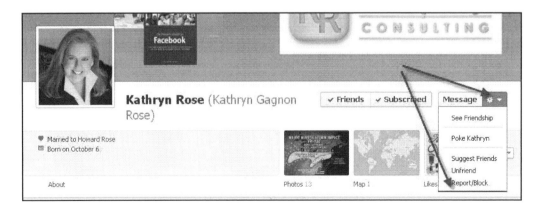

Here you have slightly different choices:

Report and/or Block This Person

○ **Unsubscribe from Kathryn Rose**
You will no longer see updates from Kathryn in your News Feed.

○ **Unfriend Kathryn Rose**
Kathryn will not be able to post on your timeline

○ **Block Kathryn Rose**
Blocking means you won't be able to see or contact each other on Facebook

Additionally, you may report this timeline as the following:

○ My friend is annoying me
○ This timeline is pretending to be someone or is fake
○ Inappropriate Cover
○ Inappropriate profile photo
○ My friend is harassing or bullying me

Is this your intellectual property?   [Continue] [Cancel]

I have also found what I call "hate pages" set up on Facebook where kids sign up for a business page or groups with the title "I Hate Jane Smith" or "I Hate Mr. Jones". They even go so far as to set up a fake profile of another kid and put their address and phone number for all to see.

If there is a hate page, fake profile or group set up with your name on it you can find it by going to the search bar and type in your name. Click on the magnifying glass to bring up all results. Then make sure to highlight "pages" or "groups." This will bring up the list of pages or groups that could have your name in the title. **These pages and groups are against Facebook's terms of use and will be taken down if they are reported.**

Here's how to report a page. Go to the offensive page and scroll to the bottom, then click 'report page'. Facebook will give you some choices about why you are reporting the page. Click the appropriate choice and then click 'submit'.

This is completely anonymous -- no one will know that you

reported the page. Don't wait to report it. There is an initiative called Stop, Block and Tell for kids on social networks. What that means is if you are being harassed, stop all communication. Your first reaction is bound to be replying and commenting back. This only gives the bully fuel and then others jump in and it becomes worse. Stop communication, then block the person through the block feature I showed you earlier, then tell someone who can help.

One thing I know for sure about bullies is that they eventually move onto someone else if you don't give them a reason to fight.

What if someone puts up a fake profile of you on the network? Take a screen shot of the page, then report it to Facebook to be deleted. You can also, from that profile or the hate page mentioned earlier, grab a screen shot of others who are members of the page and report them as well. Not everything on Facebook is anonymous.

You can also go your school and/or law enforcement. But I recommend taking a screen shot and getting the page down to minimize the damage these fake profiles can cause. Sometimes bullies put up fake profiles and include the victim's home address and other contact information, and leave the privacy settings open to "Everyone". Many people think that, like CSI and Law and Order, you can go to the school or the police and they can trace the page back to the person who created it. That may be the case, however, it is often expensive and can take a very long time. You want that page down now.

Facebook also has some resources on the site to help you in the event that you are targeted by a bully: Go to the drop down box in the top right corner, then click on Help and choose the appropriate category.

If you are being harassed to the point that you are considering taking your own life, know this: No matter what your tormentors say, the world WILL NOT be better off without you. My friend from that time is my very best friend today and we are now married to great guys, have beautiful children, and successful careers. We made it and so will you.

If you need to talk to someone, reach out. Please, please get help, here is the suicide prevention hotline, **1-800-273-TALK (8255)**, a free, 24-hour service where there are trained counselors to help you.

School systems are taking this very seriously, laws are being written to protect kids. You don't have to suffer in silence.

You also need to be aware that if you are a bully, you can and will have serious consequences when caught, including suspension and expulsion from school and possibly even criminally prosecuted. There is a case pending in Massachusetts in which two teens are being prosecuted for setting up a fake profile. And in the case where cyber-bullying caused a death, the perpetrators are being prosecuted for more serious offenses. It's not funny, it's not right. Something you did in the heat of the moment can ruin your future. Try and get into Harvard with a school suspension for bullying on your record.

I have more information on how to keep tabs on your online reputation in the "reputation monitoring" section of this book.

Chapter 11: The Wall and News Feed

What is **The Wall**?

Your 'wall' is the space on your Profile page that allows friends to post messages, write notes to you and the space where you can write posts by simply creating a 'status update'.

Each message is stamped with the time and date the message was written. Things written on your wall by you or others are published into your news feed and may be PUBLIC, unless of course you change the privacy settings so beware and make sure those privacy settings are configured properly.

The News Feed

Your News Feed (visible if you click on the "Home" link on the upper right hand side of the blue navigation bar) is a collection of your friend's posts. There are two options for viewing posts in your News Feed:

Highlighted stories are posts selected by Facebook and that show posts from your friends that Facebook thinks are most interesting to you based on your recent activity and interaction.

Recent Stories is an actual real time chronological listing of your friends latest posts presented in the "live" stream of updates. If you have established friend lists, click on the arrow next to "most recent" and then you can sort posts by friend lists. Friend lists are covered in detail in Chapter 13.

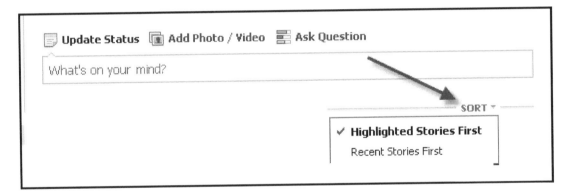

What should I post on my wall?

I'm sure if your parents were reading this over your shoulder they would say NOTHING, but you will and there is nothing wrong with interacting and having fun on Facebook. There are so many things you can post about that I think it's easier to say what NOT to post:

1. Don't post ANYTHING you wouldn't want broadcast to the world or put up on a roadside billboard. As I've said before, nothing is truly private online.

2. Don't post your vacation plans or that your parents are out of town. There was a case in the Boston area where the son posted that his parents were in Paris, a "friend" saw it and sent out party invitations to everyone in school. They did over $75,000 worth of damage to the house. There was another case recently where the mom posted that the family was going on vacation. Their next door neighbor who was a "friend" on Facebook came and robbed their house while they were gone. Tell your parents not to do post their vacation plans either.

3. Don't post pictures of yourself that are suggestive or pictures of you drinking or smoking. A "friend" could easily show them to a teacher or coach and get you in trouble at school or kicked off a sports team.

4. Don't post negative things about someone else, a classmate, teacher, your mom, brother or sister ANYONE. You wouldn't want it done to you and it is hurtful to see a

nasty post by your child. Keep your family relationships off of Facebook--that goes for Mom and Dad too!

Why don't you post about how well your team played in the game or how excited you are to be in the glee club that has an upcoming performance?

Post that you had a good time on vacation AFTER you come back, things like that.

Interacting with Posts in your Newsfeed

To interact with friends posts in the newsfeed, go to the area directly under the post and there will be displayed some options:

You can 'like' a post or 'comment' on the post. If there is a link or a photo or video the 'share' option will be visible. You can 'share' the post with your friends.

This is how you can keep in contact with your friends and stay current on their lives. You can post replies to their status updates to engage in conversation. Again, don't post anything that you want to be private.

Once you 'like' or 'comment' on a post, if other users interact with that particular post, you will get a notification.

Click on the notification and you will see that the person commented on your status or liked your status, etc.

This way you can keep tabs on the conversation.

Chapter 12: Finding People on Facebook

Now that the profile and privacy settings are done, let's move on to finding people to friend. This is probably very easy for you but I'll cover it anyway.

How do I find people? Facebook will suggest friends to you once you fill out all the information we covered in Chapter 3.

Also, if you have recently joined Facebook (or Facebook thinks you don't have enough friends) you will see a 'Find Friends' area at the top of your page:

This process is the same for both the old profile and the timeline design.

Once you click on 'Find friends' you will come to this screen:

Friends — Manage Friend List

Add Personal Contacts as Friends

Choose how you communicate with friends. See how it works or manage imported contacts.

Step 1 Find Friends   **Step 2** Add Friends   **Step 3** Invite Friends

M **Gmail**

      Find Friends

Windows Live Hotmail   Find Friends

Yahoo!   Find Friends

AOL   Find Friends

Comcast   Find Friends

Skype   Find Friends

sbcglobal.net   Find Friends

verizon.net   Find Friends

Other Email Service   Find Friends

Other Tools   Find Friends

You can find friends using their email accounts. Facebook even offers you the option to upload your email contacts and they will find friends for you. Even though they say they do not store the addresses, I never recommend uploading your contact's email addresses to any social site.

You can also click 'Other Tools' and look up by school, workplace etc.

Add Personal Contacts as Friends

Choose how you communicate with friends. See how it works or manage imported contacts.

Step 1 Find Friends	Step 2 Add Friends	Step 3 Invite Friends

	Gmail	Find Friends
	Windows Live Hotmail	Find Friends
	Yahoo!	Find Friends
	AOL	Find Friends
	Comcast	Find Friends
	Skype	Find Friends
	sbcglobal.net	Find Friends
	verizon.net	Find Friends
	Other Email Service	Find Friends
	Other Tools	

Upload Contact File
Find Friends, Classmates and Coworkers »

facebook   Kathryn Rose   🔍

Once you have done this you will see some results:

If the person has a common name like "Susan Miller," there can be a large number of results. So you'll want to filter by location, school or workplace and click "filter results."

Once you find the person you are looking for, click on 'add friend' and the person will be notified they have a pending friend request.

If you have been on Facebook for a while and have a good number of friends, the 'Find friends' option will not be shown on your page. If you have the old design, go to the 'Home' section and you can find friends either from the "people you may know" area on the right of the page, or the "find friends" area on the left:

In the new timeline design you will need to go to the timeline page (click on your name in the upper right)then click 'Friends'.

From here you click, 'Find friends' and you will be allowed to type in different bits of information to find new friends:

Find friends from different parts of your life

Use the checkboxes below to discover people you know from your hometown, school, employer and more.

Hometown

Enter a city

Current City

Enter a city

High School

☐ : _____ High School

Enter another high school

Mutual Friend

☐ Scott _____

Enter another name

College or University

☐ _____ College

Enter another college or unive...

Employer

☐

Enter another employer

Graduate School

Enter a college

+1 Add Friend

+1 Add Friend

+1 Add Friend

+1 Add Friend

+1 Add Friend

Chapter 13: Creating Friend Lists

Facebook offers a great way to organize your friends into various groups. For example, you can create a list that contains your family members, another list for your friends from a book club, or another that contains members of your soccer team. The added advantage of creating lists is that each list can be assigned different privacy setting.

A couple of notes about friend lists:

✓ You can place any friend into multiple Friend Lists.

✓ You can have unlimited number of Friend Lists.

✓ Each Friend List can have a different privacy setting.

Creating Friend Lists:

This is the same procedure for both the old and timeline designs. Go into your News Feed area and on the left click lists:

Facebook has taken the liberty to begin to create friend lists for you. Most likely you will see a list called 'Close Friends' and if you have entered family members, you will see a list named 'Family.'

If you click on the 'more' link you can create or edit your friend lists.

You will be able to create a new Friend List by clicking on the 'Create List' link.

When you click on the 'Create New List' link, a window will pop up asking you to name your list. Give your new list a descriptive name to help you identify it later. Once you create the list, you click on 'Add friends':

Test list
Custom list

Update Status Add Photo / Video Ask Question

What's on your mind?

Add friends to this list to see their updates
If you want to remove friends from the list later, click Manage List, above.

This will bring up a list of your friends. Clicking on a friend's name or picture will add them to the list, and their entry will now have a blue box with a checkmark around it to indicate that they have been selected as members of this list.

When you've selected all the friends for your list, click the done button to complete the process. This List is now added to your "Lists."

For example, I have a list named "Key Contacts" so when I go to my friends area I can click on "Key Contacts," only friends on that list will be shown.

Using Friend Lists:

You can create as many friend lists as you wish.

Facebook offers you to sort your news feed to either 'Highlighted stories' or 'Recent stories'. If you only want to see the updates from your friends in a particular list, you simply click on the list name and only the updates from the people in that list in will be displayed the in the newsfeed area.

For example, you could create a list for classmates, family, close friends, associates from a club or organization and so on — and any time you wanted to check in with that group, you could do so very easily from your Home page without having to sort through lots of other posts.

The other way to use the lists is in setting your profile privacy settings. Remember the "customize" option when setting up your privacy settings?

You can see here that "specific people" allows you to enter a "name or a LIST".

You can even use friend lists when you do status updates. On the 'What's on your mind? area, there is an area to select which people you want to view this post.

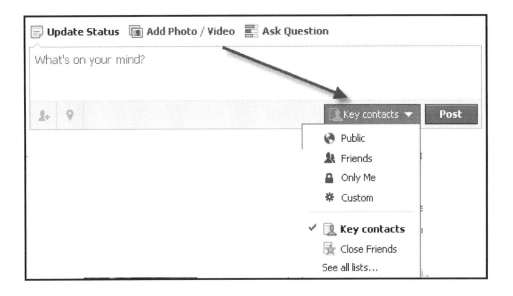

From here you can select anything you wish including a list.
You can also click the list name on the left side and it will bring
up a custom window so that your post will ONLY go to the
people on that list:

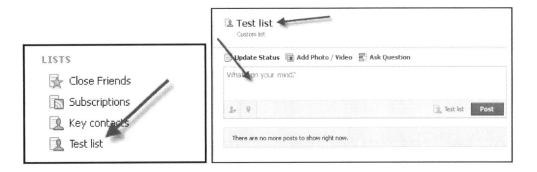

When you first sign up for Facebook or change to the new
timeline design, your post display choice always defaults to
'Public' so be sure to go in here and select either a list, 'friends'

or something to make your posts more private. Your status updates will always go back to the last setting you chose.

You can also add any friend to any list by simply going to your list and clicking on it, then clicking 'manage list', then add friends and typing in or select their name.

Chapter 14: Should I Accept A Friend Request?

So many kids think that they if they have hundreds, or even thousands of friends they will look popular. I know I would have thought the same thing. But online you have to protect your information. I've mentioned this previously but I think it bears repeating. Facebook operates on the honor system. Meaning anyone, including predators, can set up a Facebook page with a profile picture of a cute young boy and claim they're 13. It happens-- believe me it does. So if you're not careful about who you friend, you could be giving away a whole lot of information you wouldn't normally give out in person.

You might not think that someone who doesn't know you at all would even want to friend you, but it happens all the time. I get friend requests from total strangers every day.

Friending people: Very simply, do not accept friend requests from people you don't know. Period. But I live in the real world so here's my recommendation in the event you decide to ignore my advice:

When you receive a friend request from someone you don't know, the first thing you should do is take a look at their profile.

Is it public? How do you know them? Do your homework just as you would before inviting someone into your home.

When someone sends you a Friend Request you will be notified:

From there you have two choices; either accept the friend request or click "not now."

If you click "not now" This puts the person's friend request in to an area called "Hidden Requests." Don't worry; the person doesn't get a notification telling them you put them there. You can confirm the person later if you wish, and in the meantime if they go to your profile, they will just see that they are "awaiting friend confirmation".

Once you click 'not now' another screen appears, letting you know that the request has been hidden and it asks if you know this person.

Ellen
Request hidden. Do you know Ellen outside of Facebook?
Yes · No

If you indicate that you don't know the person, this will block them from trying to friend you in the future.

PLEASE NOTE: If your privacy settings are set to 'friends of friends' or 'everyone (public)', in the event someone sends you a friend request and you click 'not now' that person still may be able to see your posts in their news feed and other parts of your profile. Be cautious when using the 'not now' option, and always double check your privacy settings.

If you decide for some reason to accept a friend request later you can find them in the "hidden requests" area. To go to the "hidden requests area" go to the friend area on the top of your Facebook page (icon looks like a shadowed image of two people). Then click on "see all friend requests". From there you can again decide whether or not you want to accept the request.

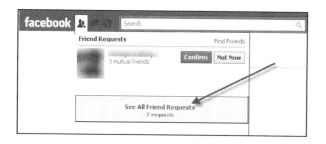

Un-friending people:

If someone you "friended" turns out to post 100 times a day or you decide you don't want to be Facebook friends with them anymore, you can "unfriend" them.

Un-friending people using the old design:

Go to your profile page by clicking on your name in the uppe

right corner. Then click on the person's name:

This will bring up the person's profile. Click on 'friends' and then 'unfriend'.

Again, the person will not be notified. But, if they go to their own friend list or try and click on your profile, they will notice that you are either missing or they cannot access your profile.

Un-friending people on the new timeline design:

Similar to the procedure in the old design, simply click on the person's name and you will be taken to their timeline:

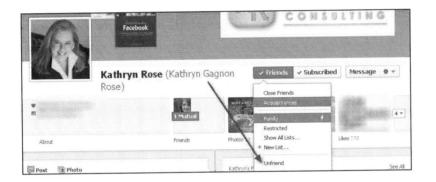

Click on 'unfriend' and they will be removed from your friend list.

Chapter 15: The New Timeline Things to Watch For

As I mentioned in the beginning of this book, Facebook has started to roll out a new design called 'timeline'. The timeline allows anyone to easily access old posts, videos and photos I've uploaded simply by clicking on a year on the right side:

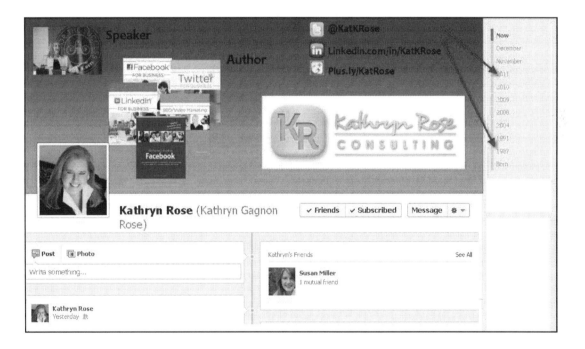

I suggest once you upgrade to the new design, you take some time to go through your old posts and either remove them completely from the site, or hide them from your timeline if you do not feel they represent you in a good light or perhaps there was a personal post you made that you'd rather not have new friends see or easily access.

If you have been on Facebook for many years, like I have, this can be very time consuming. It takes a lot of time to sort through each post and decide not only if you want it to be shown, but to whom. Many times, Facebook has changed the setting on old posts to 'public' meaning anyone who comes to your profile or timeline page can see the post.

Take these questions I answered in 2011:

Kathryn Rose | Timeline | 2011 | Highlights

Earlier in 2011

Kathryn Rose answered 6 questions.
March 28 - October 5

I am cleaning up my Facebook friends... let me know if u would like to stay....
Yes

Which type of social media personality drives you crazy?
The Over-Sharer: I don't care about what you had for breakfast.

Summer Travel Tuesday Poll Question: Pool or Beach?
Beach

Show all (6)

Apparently I did not remove them from my timeline so when I went and did a 'view as' and looked at how my profile was viewed by the public, these showed up. Now these questions are not anything that I would be embarrassed if someone read, however, I want to keep all of my profile or timeline posts private.

To remove something from your timeline, hover your mouse over the right side of the post (Facebook doesn't make it easy to find this), then click 'edit/remove'.

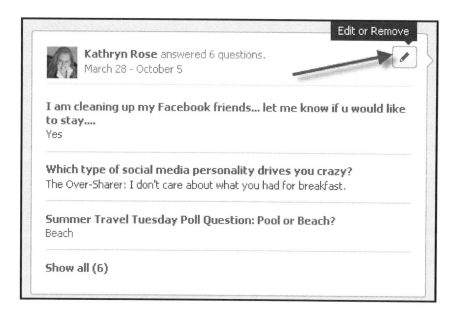

Then click 'remove from timeline'. This way no one can see this post on my timeline.

To easily view all of your posts and information you've shared on Facebook, click the 'Activity Log' link on your profile page.

This will bring up a screen ONLY YOU can see that is a complete list of everything you've shared from today back to when you joined Facebook. You can go through each and every post, photo, etc. and decide if you want it displayed on the timeline and change the security of the post.

For example:

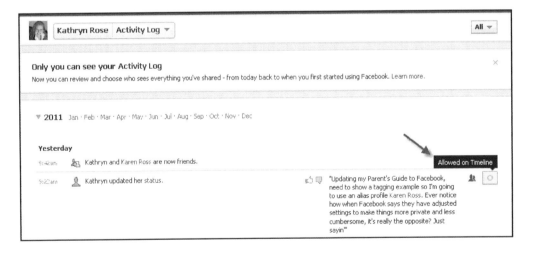

I can click on the circle next to the post and decide whether or not this can be allowed on my timeline. An open circle means that it is visible on the timeline. A circle with a line through it means it is not. You can also 'star' a piece of content and let it be featured on the timeline.

I can also click on the symbol next to the post and decide the privacy setting of who can view it:

Chapter 16: Subscribing to Updates

With the latest updates, Facebook now allows you to 'subscribe' to people's updates even if you're not friends with them. For example, a famous author or movie star may have a personal profile on Facebook but only share some information publicly. By using the 'Subscribe' option you can see what they are posting publicly in real time without having to go to their wall or timeline to view it.

If you are friends with someone you are automatically subscribed to their updates.

Because of this option, it bears repeating how important it is to be sure that your status updates are not being shared publicly or with 'everyone'. If you do not pay attention to this feature someone could 'subscribe' to your updates and see what you are doing even if you are not friends with them.

Whether you are friends or not, you can subscribe to certain updates and not others. By hovering your mouse over the 'subscribed' area, you can see the different types of information and posts that you are indicating you want to receive in your newsfeed.

You can also unsubscribe from this person's updates. This does not remove them from your friend list, just removes their updates from your news feed.

Chapter 17: Reputation Monitoring

If you hope to get a job or go to prep school or college someday, this chapter is a must read. As I mentioned earlier, admissions counselors and employers are the first ones to go to Google and type in your name once they receive your application. Using these tools to monitor your reputation will help you keep track of who is mentioning your name on the internet.

FREE SITES

Google Alerts is a great free tool that emails you automatically when there are new Google results for your search terms. You can set up a Google alert for your name, your child's name or any subject where you want regular alerts. Google currently offers alerts with results with these categories: Everything, News, Blogs, Video, Discussions and Books.

I recommend when you set up alerts, you set it to "Everything". Also, when you type your name or the name you want to set as the alert, be sure to use all variations of your name including nicknames. The best way to set up the alerts is in **quotes**. For example "Your Name" this way you will get only alerts that include both of the words YOUR and NAME as one phrase. Otherwise, you could end up receiving alerts on any time someone mentions YOUR or NAME. In my case, case, Kathryn Rose, I'd get notified every time someone mentioned the name Kathryn or the name Rose. That could be overwhelming and not useful.

How to set up Google Alerts:

Go to http://www.google.com/alerts

Google Alerts	
Search query:	"Kathryn Rose"
Result type:	Everything
How often:	Once a day
How many:	Only the best results
Deliver to:	
CREATE ALERT	Manage your alerts

You can set this up so alerts are sent to your own email or set it up through a GMAIL account. You can set up multiple alerts for the same name across different categories if you like.

PAID SITES

There are many sites on the internet now to help you monitor your reputation. "Reputation Defender" is one of the sites I have found that does this for a fee and is much more in depth than Google Alerts.

Find it at http://www.reputationdefender.com

Search Facebook

You can also search Facebook to see if someone is talking about you. To do this go to the search bar, type in your name between quote marks, hit enter then when the page comes up make sure you go to the bottom and click 'public posts'. This will bring up a search in real time of people talking about anyone with your name.

Remember though, this only includes posts by people who have their wall settings configured to 'everyone' or 'public' if someone has their privacy settings up you won't see it.

Chapter 18: Should I Friend My Mom/Dad?

This is every child's nightmare! Mom and Dad are on Facebook. As a parent, I say "yes!" of course friend them. But I know it's a concern for all teenagers on Facebook.

All I can say is you should talk with your parents about you joining Facebook and how important it is to have some privacy but understand their responsibility to protect you. After reading this book you will have all the tools you need to set your profile and privacy settings up properly. Show them you can be responsible with the technology then you don't have to worry whether or not they are hovering around in cyberspace.

You can also talk with them about appropriate behavior online and ask them to promise not to embarrass you like these parents did in these examples from myparentsjoinedfacebook.com:

Son → George ▇ Turns out it only takes 5 minutes to ride to campus and find my class. I could have slept an extra 20 minutes, gah life is hard
📱 6 hours ago via Facebook for iPhone · Comment · Like

Dad → George ▇ Young people these days, when I was in college, we had to walk 2 hours (up hill both ways) in rain, sleet, snow, 30 below 0. If it wasn't that, it was constant rain, with cars splashing tsunamis over you. If is wasn't that, then it was over 100 degree's and there was not bottled water or bottle shaped shaped water carriers, so we had to carry old army canteens which we could only fill from scuzzy dirty water fountains that were for undergrads (the best fountains were set aside for faculty and grad students). You just don't how good you have it. If we had an hour or two between classes, we could go to the student union – but it had mall cops and they'd kick you out if you weren't buying anything. How's that for hard life?
14 minutes ago · Delete

Between You and David ▇

David ▇ November 13 at 9:00am
ok Addie, you don't have to add me. But I still want to be your friend.

Share with them what you've learned and help them get their accounts set up correctly. Facebook can be a great place for you to communicate and connect with your family. I can tell you that it does hurt a parent when they are not friended or are "unfriended" by their child or their child posts hateful things about them on Facebook. Use good judgment and keep a sense of humor with your parents. Just like you, they are bound to do some stupid things (on or off Facebook).

Chapter 19: Uploading Photos and Videos

One of the most fun things you can do with Facebook is share photos and videos. With Facebook photos you can:

> **Upload unlimited numbers of photos.**

> **Create photo albums.**

> **Post comments on your friends' photos and albums.**

> **Set privacy settings for individual <u>albums</u>, limiting the groups of users that can see an album.**

> **Download photos you would like to keep.**

There are a couple of different ways to upload photos and videos. The process is the same for both (photos AND videos).

To do a quick photo post, go to your status update box and click on 'add photo/video'. You can then decide who you want to share the photo with by clicking on the drop down menu next to 'post'.

You can find Photos on the old design by clicking on the "Photos" link under your profile picture. On the new timeline design, you will click on the photo area under your 'cover' photo:

In either design, click on add photos or add videos to upload a new photo or album. Or in your own photo array, you will see that each photo is tagged by its name.

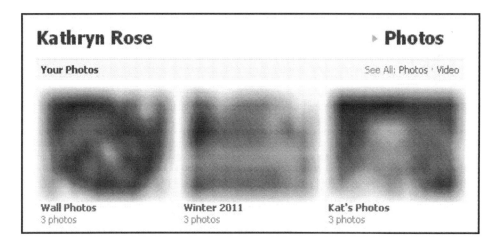

If you already uploaded an album or a photo, click on the name, and then you will see an option to "Edit Album" located on the righ side. Click on "Edit Album Info" and be taken to a screen where you can make privacy adjustments (photo below).

You can customize privacy settings for each of your photos and/or for entire albums.

You also have the ability to 'tag' or label people in a photo. For instance, if a photo features one of your Facebook friends, then you can tag or identify that friend in the photo. This sends a notification to that friend telling them they have been tagged, and provides them with a link to see the photo.

Tagging Photos of People:

As I mentioned in a previous chapter, Facebook offers users the ability to "tag" or label users in a photo. For instance, if a photo contains a user's friend, then the user can tag the friend in the photo. This sends a notification to the friend that they have been tagged, and provides them a link to see the photo.

To 'tag' someone in a photo, just click on 'Tag Photo' –

Then click on your friends face. A box will appear, place it on your friends face and you will see "type any name":

Click on the photo to start tagging.   Done Tagging

You can begin to type your friend's name, and then choose from the list by clicking on the name. You can only tag people if they are your friend on Facebook.

When your friends are tagged in your photo, they will receive the notification that they have been tagged in a photo including the link to the photo they have been tagged in. They will have the option to "remove tag" if they don't want to be identified.

Once you are done uploading the pictures, tags and description, at the bottom of the page you'll see a "Save Changes" button. Click that button, go to the top of your page and click "Publish Now" if you're ready. You can also choose to skip that step and not publish right now. Your album will be saved and you can publish it later.

Once you click "publish" your photos go out into your News Feed and are published to your profile.

Sharing Your Photos

You can share this album with your friends on Facebook by clicking the 'share' link.

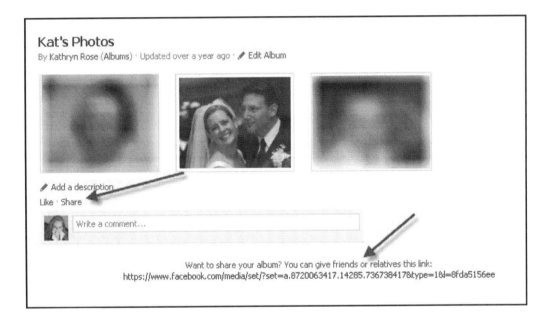

You can also share this public link with folks outside of Facebook by copying and pasting the link at the bottom of the album page.

Un-tagging Yourself from Photos/Videos:

People can post photos of you without your permission. You can ask the person to remove a photo that you do not think is flattering but they do not have to if they do not want to. One of the ways to mitigate any potential embarrassment is to un-tag yourself from photos. This doesn't remove the photo from Facebook, but if someone doesn't know you by your face, it won't identify you to the world.

Go into the 'photo' area on your main profile page. Select the photo on which you would like to remove the tag and click 'Remove/Report' tag under the picture. Once you remove the tag, it is removed from the picture, even if the photo appears in your friend's feed.

Facebook then gives you the option of saying why you want the tag removed:

If you simply want the tag removed click the appropriate area and click 'continue', and then you can decide if you just want the tag removed, you can ask the person who posted the photo to take it down or block the person who posted the photo:

Final Words

I hope that I helped you engage online with your friends, extended family and colleagues by giving you the inside track to Facebook.

Be sure to have the conversation with your parents about your activities on Facebook. It's okay to bring things up that are happening online, because it is just another place where you *all* hang out. The online communities are just a bit larger and the messages travel faster, so the importance of learning proper and safe usage right from the beginning is heightened.

I expect that you will have a great experience on Facebook and as you use it on a daily basis, you will become more comfortable and most of all have fun with it!

Facebook Glossary of Terms

Application -These are third party plug ins to Facebook that allow you to do various activities such as games.

Default settings – widely used by websites everywhere, default settings on Facebook refer to the privacy and account settings that are automatically decided for you by Facebook until your own.

Fan Page- Now referred to as a "business" page. These are pages brands set up on Facebook to promote their business or services.

Friend – a person you are directly connected to on Facebook. You accept friend requests and now this person can see your information and interact with you.

Groups- These allow you to create a group of people who all are interested in talking about the same things i.e. a book club group or a sports team group. You can set different privacy levels for different groups.

Lists - You can use this feature to organize your Facebook friends by category. For example, glee club, soccer team, family, etc. You can then sort your "newsfeed" by a friend list so you don't have to sort through lots of other posts to keep up with a particular group of people.

Messages – represented on the top of the dashboard by a message bubble-like icon. This is the area where you can send PRIVATE messages through Facebook to another user. You do not necessarily need to be Facebook friends with someone in order to send them a private message.

Newsfeed - This is where you land when you login to Facebook. It is a collection of all of your friend's posts. You will also see all of the comments, posts and interactions of your friends, the groups you belong to and the pages you like.

Notification – Facebook's way of letting you know someone posted a comment or a "like" on a post you made or if a friend has created an event. There are lots of notifications used on Facebook. To find notifications, click on the "world" symbol on the Facebook dashboard.

Poke- This is not a widely used feature on the system. You can poke someone to remind them to contact you. You cannot send a message with a poke so I don't recommend using it.

Profile/Timeline- This is the area that shows your photo, about me, relationship etc. you do not land on this page when you login to Facebook but this is where you can change details about you or place a post on your wall.

Tagging- This is the ability to identify someone in a post, video or a photo that you share on Facebook. Once the photo or post is tagged, a notification goes to the person that you have identified. You can only tag people that you are Facebook friends with, use caution and don't tag people in photos that are inappropriate.

Wall – This refers to the area on your "profile" page where people would come to leave you a PUBLIC Facebook message such as a birthday greeting.

Privacy Setting Checklist

☐ Check the "Info" page of the profile (or 'about' area) on the new timeline), edit the information to remove full birthdate, hometown and current city and any other contact information that is not necessary to have displayed. Be sure the privacy settings on your address, IM screen name, email and phone are either Friends only or only me.

☐ Go to 'Account Settings' and be sure the account security settings are configured to 'Secure Browsing' and 'login notifications' is turned on.

☐ Go to the 'Privacy Settings' area, click 'How you connect' and change those settings to your comfort level

☐ To be sure and get to review all tags made of you on the platform, go to 'How Tags Work' and set the review option to 'On'

☐ Go into the "Apps and Websites" area and edit the settings where it says "Info accessible through your friends" and uncheck all private informaiton.

☐ Go to 'privacy settings' and limit the audience for past posts

☐ If you are on the timeline design, be sure to click 'activity log' and check the settings of each post and remove ones you do not want visible on the timeline

☐ Set a "Google alert" on your name

☐ Be sure to go back into the privacy settings area every 30 days, Facebook adds and changes privacy settings fairly regularly.